OLDEST MORTAL MYTH

Oldest Mortal Myth

poems

Joanna Pearson

Story Line Press | *Pasadena, CA*

Layout by Nicolas Niño

ISBN 978-1-58654-370-9 (tradepaper)
      978-1-58654-080-7 (casebound)

The National Endowment for the Arts, the Los Angeles County Arts Commission, the Ahmanson Foundation, the Dwight Stuart Youth Fund, the Max Factor Family Foundation, the Pasadena Tournament of Roses Foundation, the Pasadena Arts & Culture Commission and the City of Pasadena Cultural Affairs Division, the City of Los Angeles Department of Cultural Affairs, the Audrey & Sydney Irmas Charitable Foundation, the Kinder Morgan Foundation, the Allergan Foundation, and the Riordan Foundation partially support Red Hen Press.

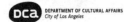

Second Edition
Published by Story Line Press
an imprint of Red Hen Press
www.redhen.org

ACKNOWLEDGMENTS

The author would like to thank the editors of the following publications in which these poems originally appeared:

14 by 14: "Navel-Gazing"; *Able Muse*: "Santa Maria della Concezione dei Cappuccini" (as "Bone Builders"), "October Inlet Wedding," and "Fashion Canzone"; *Asheville Poetry Review*: "Bells"; *Bellevue Literary Review*: "Defect"; *Best New Poets 2005*: "Personals"; *Best New Poets 2010*: "After a Molar Pregnancy"; *Blackbird*: "Epithalamion" and "The Dream Animals Long to Return"; *Boxcar Poetry Review*: "Caution Exotic Animals"; *burntdistrict*: "The Knife-Thrower's Wife"; *Cave Wall*: "Teleopsia/Pelopsia" and "Prosopagnosia"; *First Things*: "After the Mighty Gods Depart"; *Gargoyle*: "The Ice Sculptor's Wife" (as "The Ice Sculptor"); *The Greensboro Review*: "Hephaestus"; *Gulf Coast*: "The Sword Swallower's Wife"; *The Innisfree Poetry Journal*: "Heart" and "Ministrations"; *Kestrel*: "Foxes"; *Linebreak*: "Comforting Philomela"; *Literary Imagination*: "Tick"; *Measure*: "Tubercular Romance" and "Palinopsia"; *The Nervous Breakdown*: "After Icarus"; *The New Criterion*: "Minotaur"; *PANK*: "Origins of Winter" (including untitled introductory poem); *River Styx*: "Communion" and "The Mother of the Conjoined Twins Explains"; *Subtropics*: "The Body as a Condensed History of Commerce"; *Tar River Poetry*: "Anatomy"; *Unsplendid*: "The Shooter" and "The Smallest Woman in the World"; *Urbanite*: "The Munchkin Coroner Returns to Oz"; *Valparaiso Poetry Review*: "The Conjoined Twins"; *Waccamaw*: "Leda" and "Pasiphaë."

An enormous thank you to the West Chester University Poetry Center. Many thanks to all those who have supported my writing: to the Creative Writing Program and English Department at UNC-Chapel Hill, especially to Michael McFee and Dr. Stumpf; to the Writing Seminars at Johns Hopkins University, specifically to Dave Smith, Mary Jo Salter, John Irwin, and Greg Williamson; to the Corporation of Yaddo; and to the Bread Loaf Writers' Conference. Thanks to Mary Lattimore and my brother Lane for long having been my two most faithful readers. Thanks to my brother Alex and my sister Adrienne for all their love and support. Endless thanks, of course, to my Mom, Dad, Nana, and Grandaddy. And, last but never least, to Matthew.

Contents

"Old spit-up that collects inside"   11

I

Leda   15

Hephaestus   16

Pasiphaë   17

Minotaur   18

Ariadne Wakes on Naxos   19

Comforting Philomela   20

After Icarus   22

Origins of Winter   24

After the Mighty Gods Depart   30

Minor Prophets   31

Santa Maria della Concezione dei Cappuccini   33

Bells   34

The Faith Healer's Daughter   35

Communion   37

II

The Half-Lady   39

The Conjoined Twins   40

The Knife-Thrower's Wife   42

The Sword Swallower's Wife   43

The Ice Sculptor's Wife   44

The Juggler's Wife · 46

The Smallest Woman in the World · 47

De Wallen, Amsterdam · 49

Caution Exotic Animals · 50

Epithalamion · 51

Fashion Canzone · 52

The Body as a Condensed History of Commerce · 55

III

Anatomy · 59

Heart · 61

Palinopsia · 62

Teleopsia/Pelopsia · 63

Prosopagnosia · 64

Akinetopsia · 65

Achromatopsia · 66

The Munchkin Coroner Returns to Oz · 67

Tubercular Romance · 68

Ministrations · 69

Defect · 70

After a Molar Pregnancy · 72

Ascites · 73

The Shooter · 74

IV

The Mother of the Conjoined Twins Explains   79

Messages   81

Animal Afterlives   82

Metamorphoses After a Plane Crash   83

Foxes   84

The Dream Animals Long to Return   85

Tick   86

Personals   87

October Inlet Wedding   90

Navel-Gazing   91

Old spit-up that collects inside
a rock, cold tears a mountain cried,
the river's teeth, the sapling's heel,
a soup— the poor man's cunning meal,
hard trinkets that the body forms
in the gallbladder, an August storm's
contrary burst of biting ice.
We were together only twice

before I felt within my bones
that as the ancient hillside groans
raw-open to its granite king,
your kiss spoke of another thing:
dim underworld interiors,
the ceilings closing in with quartz.

I

Leda

In the most beautiful rape story
he comes as a swan.
Above her, wings beat hard,
spreading the scent of muck and lake.
Then there's a parting squawk,
arc of his neck almost apologetic
as he takes off.

But in the worst—and this
will always be the case—
she is shivering and has
your little sister's face,
an old pillow pressed
into her mouth: musty taste
of feathers, mildewed heat,
choking cough.

No longer do they break
with gravity—no lift,
no odd, consoling courtesy—
nor do they feign
the half-shyness of those
who metamorphose
for cloaked purposes
yet still take the shapes,
the dark prerogatives, of gods.

Hephaestus

Mountain-flung one, shunned son,
after his original fall from the angles
of clouded Olympus, the halls
radiant with gods, he grasped anvil and tongs.
Red-eyed old cuckold, he loved Love and lost
to big-armed War with his confident talk.
But there's solace in making.
Although children cry, lovers squint,
and girls turn away when they pass him,
he stokes blue husks of flame, lets ash waft
to his mouth. Caressing rough prongs
of ore, he draws out its glow, culling brief sparks;
with blunt blows and turning, he urges a form
to every cold desire of iron.
He's patron of all who ever make
something of beauty and, in so doing,
surprise themselves: the horse-faced seamstress
sighing as she smoothes out the silk,
a fermata quavering in the blind bluesman's throat,
an old man quaking at his beautiful daughter.

Pasiphaë

"You treat me like a big, warm beast," he said
when I last pulled him softly to my bed
to comfort me. I wouldn't be alone.
Mornings, I took the cool seat of my throne.
My king would sigh and rub his weary brow.
"How did you sleep?" he'd ask. I'd shrug. "And how
about yourself, my lord?" He'd twist his ring
while coughing, nod, and tell the servant, "Bring
a plate of fruit and bread for us to eat."
I'd pluck some grapes. We'd breakfast, cold and neat.

My appetites were other, anyhow,
those full-mooned evenings, dressing like a cow.
The white bull's nostrils misted in my hand,
his muscled shoulders wider than a man's.
He'd nuzzle, heave his shaggy forelimbs, gentle
for a thing so large and elemental.
It wasn't odd, the urgent fur and grunting,
just two creatures in the moonlight rutting;
seemed natural, in fact, to lie beneath
those dainty, cloven hooves. His cud-stained teeth
revealed themselves in love's crude, closing sneer,
and then we'd rest. I'd curl and nestle near
his steamy rump, my headrest his long spine.
Who knew then there'd be labyrinth or twine,
or youth sent down as useless sacrifice
for my rough son? Yet nothing will suffice
to quench my husband's anger, after all—
our instincts, in the end, still animal.

MINOTAUR

He's formed wrong-halved,
uniquely, unlike the people-faced
hybrid creatures: muscled centaurs,
foliage-shaded satyrs,
sleek mermaids weaving water,
flicking light with iridescent tails.
He bears his heavy cow head
above shivering human knees
and mollusk-soft genitals.
Misfit of the half-breeds,
he shames, reminder always
of the royal wife crouched, lowing
in moonlight for her stud bull.
It's no wonder he's bitter
in that stained labyrinth littered
with dry bones, the stench
rising from blood-matted fur,
animal-heat misting from his nostrils.
He hates as one can only hate
when others are repulsed.
The Athenian youth are sent,
bedewed and draped in terror,
and his halfling heart beats faster.
They scream at his approach.
He grunts, distressed again,
then devours them—
but watch with what slow tenderness
he pauses, dismembering
each lovely, sweet-fleshed woman.

Ariadne Wakes on Naxos

New love is like jug wine: you wake up hard
and headachey, or in a sour pool
alone, strange trees all trembling overhead.
The black-winged ship turned tiny as a toy,
she sits to rub her gritty eyes, regard
the island's flitting forms as they unspool
beyond her grasp like water-colored thread.
Recall the labyrinth; that tawny boy

from somewhere else who looked at her and smiled;
her hidden brother in his nest of bone,
sword-struck, stumbling, calling like he knew.
Yet still she longs for him who so beguiled
her thoughts that right and wrong were overthrown
or blurred, like where he sails, to blue on blue.

COMFORTING PHILOMELA

After raping Philomela, Tereus "seized her tongue
with tongs and, with his brutal sword, cut it away."
—Ovid

I kiss her, and her hands flit up like toys,
like white doves into the air. Light falls
across her bony shoulder, forming a false
bandolier. She gently mouths no-noise,

twists cracked lips until vibrations thrum
within the hollow of her throat. Silence
breaks—she keens, a human theremin.
I pull her close, pausing to glance

at every plum-dark bruise, the stump of tongue,
her emptied velvet mouth. She stares at me.
I touch her neck where words must be
shuttered within. Climbing each rung

of ribs, my fingers seem to understand
what she wants and is. But she reaches for a pen,
shaking her head, and grabs my hand,
writes, "Nightingale." In the windowpane,

a bird sights its reflection, strikes,
dizzying itself; hops back to revise
its angle, strike again. Her wet eyes
flicker brownly, then overfill, streaks

of mascara blackening each cheek.
We sit listening to the sound of a small
body battering glass, its thwarted music. Speak
to me, I plead. She shivers as we fall

together on the bed, yet holds me like a child,
stroking my hair, rubbing my brow. I whisper
sweet gibberish to her wounds, kiss her
like she's a creature broken and made mild,

until she flies from me, a feathered thing,
and I'm left clutching scraps of dawn, of nothing.

After Icarus

His father wept and bore
a distance swimmer's ache
in his neck and shoulders.
He avoided old haunts,

found new ones, but
the tale had spread there, too.
He accepted free drinks
nodding barkeeps offered.

He tried discussing weather
with sullen-eyed strangers
who saw his grieving face
and moved outside to smoke.

Young men above their cues
seemed ghost-like but less beautiful.
From a booth he'd watch them
shattering rounds of triangles.

He saw the world in parts
down to its very atoms
and dreamt persistent dreams
of breast stroking through cumulus,

green sea daubed with feathers,
water and wax emulsion.
He'd wake with bleeding lips
and new knots in his muscles.

(With wings, who couldn't lose
himself, soaring like
a bored god? Like light,
both wave and particle?)

He let himself be babied
by loose women who held him
to their bosoms, kissed his ears,
whispered, *Hush, sweet mister.*

For years, he wore dark lenses,
shunned the bloody sunrise,
forgot that when he'd landed
he'd knelt before the brightness.

Origins of Winter

I. WE MEET

I am the honey-limbed girl dropping wet petals
along the path, careless with beauty in the way
of the young; suggestive. Before dusk settles

in the cleft of distant hills, I weigh
my options: return home before dark,
or watch slow clouds like servants lay

a ruby into the arms of trees, a spark
reddening sweetly in its slip of sky.
Waiting until the sun completes its arc,

earth shivering beneath me, I feel shy—
alone but for the murmur of crickets who note the air
cooling, whispers of a stream, the sigh

of leaves still lost in gossip, Who's there?
Who's there? That pretty thing? Fireflies dart
around my ankles, brash, trying to nibble where

no man has yet. And ripping earth apart,
you emerge, root-gnarled, all mineral and sweat.
Your horse snorts as you present a heart . . .

or pomegranate dripping from your hand of jet,
skull burning through your translucent face.
I cringe, aware the offer is a threat.

Careful, I lift my cheek for your embrace,
inhale your scent of calcium and ash.
The cut fruit stains my arm as we retrace

your route on our descent through that new gash
of rocky clay. Down. Down. The underworld.
You raise a casual arm to show your cache

of shimmering jewels, colors ruddy, swirled
against the cavern walls by flickering light
from high torches. A tablecloth's unfurled

across a marble slab. I have no appetite,
but food appears: cheese, Muscat grapes, a knife.
Elsewhere, my mother will not sleep tonight,

but you are saying, *Join me, lovely. Join me, wife,*
words that sting like hail or poison nettles,
your touch like nothing I've felt in all my life.

2. SOLSTICE

Here it was always dark,
so it grew darker above ground.
My mother bit her fingernails and frowned,
letting the scenery turn stark.

Her lovely features blurred.
When asked to describe in one word

my feelings for this place,
I answered, "Neutral," but longed for blues and greens. Your face
stayed quiet as an underground pool,
and you nodded, passing me a plate.

The rule
about eating had been made clear, so the weight

of fruit rested in my palm till I declined. Overhead,
people scurried like miners, like moles.
You looked at me and pointed to your bed.
Blind fish plunging, I learned how naked skin consoles

the lonely, hidden soul you don't believe in. My bellyache
had grown ragged, wanting—something like love
but merely hunger so large that I mistake
you now for all I've lost, all I've been dreaming of.

3. PORTRAIT: A VERSION OF OUR MORTAL LIFE

When you whisper, *Hell yeah! We're gone!,*
I rehitch the fallen strap of a dress
my mother doesn't know I own,
the cheap one that reveals me when I jump into your car.
We drive to a honky-tonk off Highway 74
and scuff soles through the parking lot,
stirring up gravel. We befriend a one-armed man
named Herb, passing him beer bottles
he opens with his teeth. I blow blue-gray
wreaths of smoke around our heads, and you
stub out your cigarette against the tender part
of your wrist. We kiss like lampreys
while Herb, hooting, takes swigs and tosses
empties aside, chats up the aspiring model/actress
late to work at the bar inside. Licking her thumb,
she draws a heart in the air around us, fakes a pout
when you won't kiss her, then scampers off.
When the moon's fuzzed by clouds, Herb flicks
his ash, clears his throat, and says, *You better take
your sugar somewhere now,* nodding at us.
And *somewhere* is a patch of pasture grass,

or the last good backseat, make-out parking spot
by the railroad tracks. We move, choreographed:
worn jeans, short dress, ripped t-shirt, weather
crackling into summer storm. Rain-soaked,
our shirts meld to the surface of our chests,
we press each other in a grocery-romance-novel way.
You adore me best, and I, you; our love
rendering any threat of other love impossible
there in the bright, bad *now* of lightning
unseaming our lonely spread of sky,
uprooting the cobalt hill, undoing me and you.

4. THE SEEDS

We'd thrashed and wept in tangled sheets
enough by then to have a ritual:
you'd stroke my head and offer me
something bright, glistening—a plum
or pear steeped in sunlight from the groves
where now my mother's mourning causes leaves
to wither. I'd cup the gift
like a green world, breathing in its skin.
But I couldn't eat. I couldn't taste
that world again without dying.
So instead I'd cling to you and ask
you to make me less lonesome.
Until one day you said, *I like some flesh
on a woman. You've become a wraith.*
And I smirked, Good, then I'll fit in.
You didn't laugh but turned away—
always some business as lord of this place.
Yes, we were well-kept by your milk-eyed loyals:
there were fêtes and mummers and

dance recitals, always the limber dead
performing for our pleasure.
And time has rolled over and over
until my decision and its *why* have spread
so far apart that I cannot recall
the importance of my hunger anymore,
so shivering, near-bald, my jaw downed,
stomach shrunken hard as a peach stone,
I see glowing a halved pomegranate:
thick, tough skin, innards like red sequins.
I stroke it like a blind woman. Plucking
six seeds, I let them burst between
my teeth. My tongue's still quivering
when you walk in and laugh, drink deeply
the tart bloodstain of my mouth—drink me
like a man who's waited and grown thirsty.

5. PORTRAIT: OUR LIFE ON THE EVENING NEWS

It's always my old school photo they show:
blonde pigtails, toothy grin—what, twelve years old?
Fifteen? Last seen picking flowers . . .
at the mall . . . waiting for the school bus.
The sketched face of a man pops up,
eyes charcoaled in, jackal lines around his mouth,
a nightmare-composite. Watch how my mother
pleads in front of microphones for any tip or clue,
for the safe return of her child. Her voice is mild
with Ativan and breaks between words. The man
behind her stirs, my father, looking shamed
and puzzled (the tabloids soon will speculate
why he's not quite sad enough.) But already
I'm forgetting them—her hands, his oxford shirt,

the big clock in my classroom, my school photo,
how the photographer pulled down the blue background
and said, "You got a lotta boyfriends, sweetie, don'tcha?
Now smile! Hold it!", the white curtains in my bedroom,
and even you, sir, even you, your paper mask and dark eyes
hovering above me now as I lie sleeping. And this new place.
My absence is voracious, swallowing everything.

6. FIRST THAW

The world when I returned was caulked with ice—
a happening for which we had no word—
so now I tasted branches, the precise
mold of every twig a language that I heard
with my cold tongue and understood at last.
My mother, holy with suffering, asked if I
must lick everything. Six months had passed
and, now a guest, I blanched—we'd turned shy
and formal together. *It will melt soon
now you're back*, she said, and then the black
plate of the lake cracked as if the moon
were a hot coal. And I saw how a long-felt lack
is each thing's ghostly imprint—how ice burns,
and beauty, lost, more fervently returns.

They do not always hear our special plea,
the lame gods—Deaf-In-One-Ear, Old Hobbled-Knee,
that sooty lug the lovely naiads flee—
but sometimes we are left with them alone
to call on when the kingly ones have gone,
our household gods have slipped into the sea,
the seawalls all have crumbled into dust,
and waves sweep both the pious and unjust
into a foaming gray infinity.

What purpose in the early pantheon
did they support? While rosy-fingered dawn
massaged the contours of immortal brawn,
they rounded out the sacred coterie
with broken parts—almost humanity.
They shuddered at the thunder, faces drawn,
and turned when others made the earth combust
with lightning bolts of wanton, godly lust
and incense like smoked feathers of a swan.

Yet when the muscled mighty disappear,
we're left with them. We cry and hope they hear,
who linger, maybe, impotent and near.

Minor Prophets

I

Consider the forgotten minor prophet:
a grizzled man who spoke of covenants
broken, and locusts. The sandstorms sent to buffet
his hard cheeks distilled his penitence.

II

Your auntie notes the taste that wedding day
of moist air thickening, the cheap champagne.
With Cleopatra-ed eyes, the bride will stay
beneath that red sky blossoming with rain.

III

In April, watch the wry urologist's
plump wife lift up a frothy cherry bloom, her
slow caress cut short when he suggests
its petals look just like a bladder tumor.

IV

In smoky bluish depths, the mermaids wish
each for a shipwrecked sailor's handsome face.
They'll cradle him in kelp until the fish
nibble him to bone and doily lace.

V

Plain old granny had her bucktoothed warning
to settle down or straighten up. Behave.
She cracked her knuckles, draped herself in mourning,
then scuttled satisfied into her grave.

VI

The ragged mongerers still vitiate
this gray world from their chosen deserts, spent
with bleak foretelling. God-hungry, they wait
for rumbling voices—harsh, magnificent.

Santa Maria della Concezione dei Cappuccini

In Rome, there is a chapel made of bone—
and what ingenious builders who first saw
a second use for each remaindered part,
old planks and joints we leave when we are gone,
so built their holy spaces with an awe
for bodies' grimmest afterlife as art.

The femur makes the longest cut of timber
while slender rib bones swoop in lovely curves,
and blunt phalanges do for detail work.
The ghastly skull is there to help remember
past functions of this scaffolding, and serves
as prelude, like the shadow men who lurk

in myth collecting teeth from childhood beds
then trail us, pockets clacking, through our heads.

BELLS

Once, these bells were rung to ward off plague
and bring the faithful thronging through the doors.
Today, old ladies leave with Sunday's vague
sense of something—something that ignores
the rote confession of metallic notes
swung only rarely from the weathered tower,
beseeching no one. Nothing marks the hour.
But now and then, an antique clanging floats

above bent heads of people in the town,
who shuffle, dull-tongued, keeping their eyes down
yet sometimes whisper, find they still desire
old words, the ululations of a choir;
and notice when the birds all scatter south,
when the clapper breaks inside its burnished mouth.

THE FAITH HEALER'S DAUGHTER

In wheelbarrows and wagons people came,
anemic, wheezing, crippled, blind, or daft.
A dancer limped from cancer of the spine;
a butcher stumbled, struck by fainting fits.
Offering tea and corn bread, I explained
that Papa'd soon see each of them. Meanwhile,
I rocked slick, feverish babies in my arms,
flocked by mothers—a flurry of white moths.
Translucent-skinned old ladies pulled me down
to kiss their shriveled cheeks and dusty mouths.
Humming, I rubbed lanolin on their limbs—
massaged their hard-burled, crooked carpentry—
browned and bent from decades hunched in cotton.
They pressed my forehead with their seedpod-fingers
eagerly—I was his only daughter.
He laid his massive hands on those who knelt,
and said, *Be healed now if ye have enough*
true faith. They felt, they said, the pain
dissolving into vapor. They were healed.
I'd hide behind the curtains, watch them cry,
their streaming faces tilted toward the rafters.

Eventually they all called him a fraud,
forgetting how he'd lit rooms with his words,
burned holy from the tallow of his eyes.
The town played host to other wanderers
and lulled itself with handsome peddlers' oils.
In our bare house, my papa kissed his flask,
retired from sacred work, and rarely spoke.
Sour-breathed, he let his beard grow white and gnarled.
I heard the whispers: *Hear how the old man*
went strange and took to drink? I'd turned out odd
and angular, so plain that they forgot

the girl I'd been, the man who was my father.
When he grew ill, I nursed him those last months
the plainest way, without his radiance
or scripture, but with ice, a vial, cool cloths.
In all the years, what did I learn from him
of suffering or solace? Prayer. A hymn.
Hot broth. A touch. If needed, laudanum.
Whiskey. Ghostly angels circling us.

Communion

How not unlike Communion was first love—
you and I in the church kitchen, Sunday donuts, a dove
etched on our hymnals. You revered the law
like God, so we were hesitant when touching. We saw
each other's nakedness and knew we'd only go so far—
splayed diagonals of limbs forming a fleshy star.
One time for a joke you took the blessed econo-jug
of leftover Concord Grape, sad and store-bought. Smug,
you drank, then wiped your mouth, carnivorous, bloodstained.
Still, I took a swig. It tasted ordinary. That explained
it all. The crumbs of love were also small: denial and restraint.
You held one hand up like an Old World saint,
bowed your head, leaned closer to bestow
a kiss like the All-Mighty, who cannot be told no.

II

THE HALF-LADY

Among the jealous circus folks, she's hated—
by the fat-but-not-humongous lady,
the puny strongman, and bruised trapezer. Waited
on hand and foot by gruff, retired dwarves,
she preens, applies her powders, creams, and blush.
They fuss about her, bring her tea and scones.
She's beautiful, high-cheek-boned with the flush
of youth, straight teeth, those breasts and hips and yet
no legs—a stump of girl, torso to floor.
Her voice is bright and operatic. She drags
her body arm-by-arm in a maneuver
that she's perfected for the stage, and sings
just like an angel, they all say—the men
who go no further than cliché
in their smitten descriptions, who pay again
each day for her performance, mesmerized
and lost in love or pity. Some raise a hat
and, clapping, fling a single long-stemmed rose,
waiting for the final, drawn-out moment
that gutwrenches them each time: a handsome guy
strolls bashfully out, long-limbed, with a bouquet.
He pauses as if nervous, checks the crowd,
then kneels before their mademoiselle. He'll say,
My itty-pretty love! My demi-darling!

She'll clasp his hand. The music will then start
again, and she will gracefully deliver
her denouement that brings the crowd to tears
I may be half a person but I have—

> *a whole heart!*

She beams at them with bland, convincing joy,
and holding hands, she bows beside the actor,
then leaves to play roulette with Lizard Boy.

THE CONJOINED TWINS

We looked so lovely when, as girls, we wore
those fat, starched ribbons in our ponytails,
white matching pinafores of eyelet lace,
and coal-black patent leather boots. A pair
of beauties in cahoots, we whispered jokes,
then sang on stage in high, canary voices
our slow, plaintive duet, its innocent
refrain of love and never-lonesomeness.
They asked for autographs, the soft-voiced men
who stared with quivering hands and rheumy eyes,
and looked like they might gobble us. We shared
that uncleaved slope of skin and bone, our pelvisto-
pelvis perma-dance; like knotted gymnasts,
we shook and shimmied cute but double-wide
through doorways into spotlights with a smile
and dual curtsey, to applause, gasps.
Charmed by our pale parasols, they wept,
the wives, and whiskered gentlemen adored us,
but we yearned for the lion tamer's boy.
We wrote him love notes on blue stationery.
He kept away from us until we lured
him close with mirrored blossoms, twenty fingers
to coax him toward our slim, carnivorous petals.
He tugged our manes and gentled us like felines.
We were a two-stemmed cherry made for sharing,
but he picked only one. The smell of lions,
fur and fetid breath, would make us flinch,
but we stayed stalwart, played the melded darlings
until the end. Now our strange rest positions
remain a comfort underneath the sheets

these evenings as we hum ourselves to sleep.
Our joints are bad, our voices crack, we charm
no one at all. The carnival has gone.
We stare out separate windows of the house,
and hold a single silence, drink our tea.
When we undress for bed, we speak no words,
dream riven dreams of sharp knives glittering.

The Knife-Thrower's Wife

One must stay beautiful and lean
against that Devil's Door
or Wheel of Death, so still
one barely breathes. Lipstick,
rouge, and pantyhose transform me
nightly into the thrower's target girl,
the hushed crowd's captive darling.
A sigh and wink. Steel blinks.
My husband's white teeth
flash their signals: *confidence,
danger, beauty!* I keep my calves
taut, smile tight, eyes bright
with the sole pleasure—this desire
to be threatened but not hurt.
Metal whizzes near earlobe,
sweet hip flesh, arm cleft,
the V of spread legs, and
zing! hums in notched wood.
He's bowing to applause. I wave
slowly to the trembling child,
struck by what might have been.
A target girl must make love
to everyone and no one. Touched
by nothing but the blade's clean, almostkiss,
each intimate miss, I arrange
myself upon his board again,
supple, lovely to the risk.

THE SWORD SWALLOWER'S WIFE

Soup spoon, drum stick, pool cue—his urge began one day
out of the blue as all desires to test the body do.
He popped his neck. He no longer touched me the way he used to.
I found him gagging on the broom handle. They say
you must be patient, entice
your man back to you with old-fashioned lingerie
of ruched satin, cook for him the way
his mother once did, add a little spice
to the bedroom ritual, play peekaboo. But he grew hoarse.
There were no carrots left for the roast beef; even the curtain rod
was slimy. There was an occasional facade
of romance: him sucking my spidery fingers, but slowly, for
            much too long, of course.
I caressed the bulb of his larynx. *Watch*, he said. *I hate
this*, I whispered, turning from the blade.

THE ICE SCULPTOR'S WIFE

Yes, it was hard to be in love with him—
chapped hands and bluish lips, the chilly silences,
always an urgent temperature.
He overran my yard with great parades
of glistening horses, turreted castles,
perfectly frozen dancers, and a hundred-hundred
sharp bouquets of scentless flowers.

All of it melted, of course,
but he bedecked me in diamonds of a sort,
a hail of kisses, my neck red and numbed
under the burning star of each karat.
He carved my frosty features, reproductions.
He's a wonder with a chisel, my friends said,
blinded by their iridescent likenesses.

Meanwhile wetness crept in rivulets.
I grew to dread the dampness of our bed,
the way we woke to puddled shapes instead
of shimmering abundance, how things turned
to drip and sucking mud beneath our feet,
the air quoting its cool absences.

I spurned the calm precision of his touch,
his quick-spent carefulness, sudden figures that emerged
only to fade after hours in the sun.
I stopped serving cold drinks,
developed a preference for steam,
warm hearths, marble antiquities—

impermanent too, he countered, pointing to headless
Winged Victory and a torso of Apollo.
Decay may be just a question of speed,
but give me blood and stone, a child
of voice and bone, not the seep of brittle water.

The Juggler's Wife

We live inside the house of shattered things:
tea cups, crystal vases, china plates.
There's nothing that he sees and doesn't wish
to toss above his head in figure eights.
I walk across the carpet, mind the glass
from all my tiny headless figurines
to see if there's a book still on the shelf
whose spine's not cracked from hours loop-de-looping.
All our sharpest knives have plunged already
into our sofa's cushioned, fat-armed leather.
At night, he throws our pillows overhead
until the room's ablur in snowing feathers.
I watch him, but he's always gazing up
to catch suspended objects in their arcs,
to gauge the grasp of gravity and how
he might send every object into orbit
except toys from the child's room. They're untouched,
and like our quiet now, remain unbroken.
I press the ground, look down, and smell the soil,
earthbound, lower than his flickering eye,
which can't perceive disaster underfoot
so intent on something lovely in the sky.

THE SMALLEST WOMAN IN THE WORLD
Cleveland County Fair, Shelby, NC

We're sixteen. The air is cool and bright,
and we have driven to the Fair. The night
is pocked by speaker noise, the shouts and squeals
of funnel-cake-stuffed kids on Tilt-a-Whirls.
The tattooed carnie, drunken, with a leer,
blares Metallica and growls to us, *C'mere.*
My friend and I can't laugh. We're too afraid
of our own awkwardness now to be made
into objects—except of ridicule:
a pair of girls who look like Olive Oyl.

Despite our vintage tees and jeans preferred
by pseudo-indie kids, we're both straight nerd,
or so we seem to that cute roaming pack
of cheerleaders. Dressed brightly, they're compact
as multifunction pocket calculators
with straightened hair, lip-gloss, the matching purse.
We duck behind the Shriners' corndog stand
to hide, and watch the glowing clock face hand
of the Ferris wheel turn underneath the moon
that's risen like a looming gold balloon.

At last we spot a sign we've never seen
on a peeling, corner trailer, "Tiny Queen
Yvonne! The Smallest Woman in the World!
Royal of her tribe!" A line is curled
from the ticket-taker standing at the door.
The people whisper, curious for more
than the sign displaying a beautiful
cartoonish tiny woman with those full
breasts and lips, long hair, and kewpie eyes,
wide in playful, miniature surprise.

We line up too and wait to pay the guy,
walk in the trailer slowly, half-scared, shy.
Yvonne sits on some blankets, watching soaps.
She's old and wrinkled; fleshy. Her face slopes
downward, drooping folds like a Shar Pei.
Her joints are ringleted with fat the way
a baby's are. She smells like beer and Skoal
and underarm. She has a furred chin mole,
and yes, she is a dwarf, but not *that* small.
She glares at us. We're somber-eyed and tall,

and shame heats up our cool. With firm-set jaw,
we leave to find the long-haired boys we saw
by the 4-H sign. We pair off now to kiss
the boys, mock rides and passersby, dismiss
this *boring, stupid farce.* Our smoky lips—
detached, ironic—part, and each tongue slips
inside a clumsy, candy-appled mouth.
The four of us are coupled, making out
dank scent of cow, faint dung, that hay-filled must.
We feel the shrinking power of new lust
distill us down and Thumbelina us.

DE WALLEN, AMSTERDAM

Pale women in the windows pose for men,
smoke and sulk toward dank canals and blow
mean kisses, glare at us—American,
female, and twenty-two. The side streets show
them fatter, older, less a van Eyck hue
and more the range of milky coffee, new
arrivals to the tiered Dutch carnival.
Nervous, we can't help but pause and stare
into their eyes, kohl-dark, professional.
Beckoning, one leans and slings her hair,
then shimmies, turning backwards to the glass
to rub it gently with her g-stringed ass.
Clumps of drunken tourists laugh and shout,
pointing out the ones with whom they'll bargain.
The passed-by ladies smirk right back and pout,
feigning disappointment. We begin
to realize what we've never been before:
transparent, wholly camouflaged by more
flamboyant creatures. We're like the peppered moth
in the Industrial Revolution—drab
and safely hidden. Cutting a zigzag swath
past XXX, porn shops, and those gray slab
facades of quiet, eyeless *kerks*, we leave
the district's heart, yet still we see them wave,
some ancient alley-whores who grin and bare
their rotten teeth at us. In this old world
of grab and buy, of flesh and trade, the air
has lost its warmth, and we're unnerved, un-girled.
The moon above the spires, a sexless disk,
eyes us coolly as an odalisque.

CAUTION EXOTIC ANIMALS

Deputies hunted down lions, bears, and dozens
of other exotic animals that escaped after they
were let loose by the suicidal owner of a local
animal preserve.

Imagine this, not gunshots, not the ending,
but the giraffe's blue-gray blade of tongue
nipping Ohio air, its neck a strung bow bending
out the rusted gate, that damp lung
of hillside exhaling fur and scat and rain
while the sulky tigers paw a muscular ballet
along the glistening stripe of motorway,
the jabbering monkey thumbs a soda can,
and the black bear trundles nowhere in particular,
eyes catching in the headlights of a car.
Imagine the first stunned moment of opened cage,
that ripple of sudden animal-joy, like rage,
not the moment quiet death appeared,
not the lion, asleep on his wet beard.

EPITHALAMION

Three weeks in, the masked man whispered,
Let me disfigure you gently, as he knelt
by her bed. She seemed to nod while she dreamt.
He gathered his tools from a pouch:
chisels, dull knives, gag and stirrups,
barbs, ninja stars, tools for working leather.
Slowly, he began to skive the v of her throat,
prick her breasts till they bled, and the room
filled with ghosts and not-ghosts of children
who were, or who never would live.
They hummed in a taffy light around her head.
"You must be the devil," she wanted to say, or said.
He chuckled a bit, shucking the skin
like an old stocking from her leg, sanding raw
her forearms. "I can't see my hands," she whispered,
"or read small print. You don't exist." He laughed
again, buckling her in two. She heard herself split
like melon, too-ripe strawberry, sweet, dark fruit,
dripping down to the hard arch of her cramped foot.
Her mother's voice warned, "Always keep things clean."
But now he caressed the fine skin of her face
with a tingling. His fingers dipped and traced,
left the taste of burnt sugar. When she turned
to look, he was gone. Instead, in his place,
lay her beautiful husband, lips parted,
sleeping with a blind man's outstretched arms.

Fashion Canzone

I watch their narrow hipbones with delight,
the stubborn catwalk stalk, quick clicks I hear—
stiletto points—and shivering layers of light
chiffon on shoulder blade refracting light.
Hunched with slicked-back bun and too-tight dress
(I should have stuck to strict low-carb and lite!),
I turn a page. My Montblanc pen alights,
scribbling slender adjectives. I write
for wolfish women who observe each rite,
take cues from haute couture, glide with a light,
fevered radiance, like pinpricked stars—
their distant, empty brows, eyes fierce as stars.

She strides out now, one of those one-named stars
whose skin is luminescent with a light
that seems innate, combusting like one star
white-hot against backdrops of fainter stars.
In the crowd around me I can hear
admiring whispers from toned movie stars,
celebrities, and industry lodestars
who've come to gaze upon a pale slip dress
that's worth a small Picasso, or a dress
inlaid with jewels like a night sky set with stars.
Adjusting pantyhose, stiff-kneed, contrite,
I wish I could do more than sit and write—

but it's pathetic and, far worse, it's trite
to see these coltish beauties, runway stars,
or a tall, translucent, adolescent sprite
from the former Eastern bloc, now bright
in Prada, tooth veneers, and strong spotlight,
and want to prance up there instead of write
my article for *Vogue*. Heck, I'm all right

to those who've known me naked — blunt, austere,
no nonsense and no bullshit. I won't hear
the false romantic promises (yeah, right!).
Businesslike, I kiss, letting my dress
fall to the floor. We do our thing, then dress . . . .

Applause for the designer. His address
to us is brief. I fan my neck and write,
*Elegant yet avant-garde, his dress
recalls early Yves Saint Laurent. He'll dress
debutantes, It-girls, and all the stars.*
I pause, wish for the coolness of that dress,
against my cheek like water: small redress
for beauty's partialness. I want one light
relic of beauty, having been its acolyte.
Classic, recherché— in such a dress,
I imagine the caresses, how I'd hear
some honest passion murmured in my ear . . . .

But like the perfect falsehoods that inhere
in trompe l'oeil paintings, nothing in a dress
could make up for the actual. I hear
the girls are bleak and caffeinated here,
know nothing of love either; that they write
their mamas back in Poland, and you hear
them weeping foreign tears at night. You hear
about two or three bronzed, leggy superstars
who sprawl on every glossy page — the stars
of signs and magazines. The rest adhere
to cigarettes, champagne, Tasti-D-Lite,
and, after shows, drift ghost-like into twilight.

It ends. An ugly man offers a light,
leaning in so close that I can hear
the ticking of his Rolex, Gucci dressshirt
stiffly creasing, heavy breath — seems right
to stand with him beneath cold coins of stars.

Dear decimal digits,
                    dear numismatic skull plate,
from the first *this for that*, the ticker-tape heart rate,
you were built to buy and seize
a pound of flesh,
                    new vascular territories.
The hand, a skin-sack of metacarpal coins;
the mouth, an ATM;
                    the first parted loins
equipped for withdrawals, deposits, foreclosures,
before the bubble's burst
                    and the non-disclosures.
Our early currencies were, in truth,
quite simple:
                    an eye for an eye, a tooth for a tooth.
Or else all was accomplished by barter: tit
for tat, tit to mouth, tit for milk, bit by bit
filched from self —
                    our blastular investments
with raw returns
                    and wrenching divestments.
And in such primitive economies of gland
always the supply,
                    always the demand.

III

Anatomy

I

How peaceful, pickled bodies under tarps,
and so much less disturbing than we thought
to slice gray rind, to peel the stringy fascia,
to trace out nerves in arms as stiff as branches.
Each chest, preserved, is rubbery as latex.
The now-slack buttocks bunch, acquire the texture
of dank, pocked, day-old orange peels in dumpsters,
but underneath a glow of humming lights,
we hunch to task in plastic gowns and gloves,
and disassemble—carpentry reversed.

II

At home some evenings you and I rehearse
the names of different parts, our own landmarks,
and touching, try to make them meaningful.
I hold your hand and feel your carpal bones:
 hamate with its shepherd's hook,
 the pea-shaped *pisiform*,
 triquetrum, broad, three-cornered hat,
 lunate like a crescent moon,
 trapezium and *trapezoid*, two brothers
 tumbling in a circus act,
 capitate, a bobbleheaded boy
by the curvilinear *scaphoid* ship—
 all that inside one hot, pale wrist.

III

We've not yet learned
long litanies of diseases,
but with this art of naming, we are thus

made powerful—fierce, vivified by love.
Supinating ulnar bones, we stroke
scapulae, then clavicles. I kiss articulations
of phalangeal joints, breathe in the post-lab scent
of hair steeped sweet with formalin.

Textbooks with neat labels,
dead people wearing frozen faces,
they are nothing—not to us, not to our promises,
nor to these early moments in the etymology
of quickening love, when we seek to carve
that oldest mortal myth of permanence through words.

Heart

My mother, thinking that her heart would burst,
sank softly, pale, between the grocery aisles,
still clawing at a half-filled shopping cart.
Cool drifts of wordless jazz continued faintly
through bright ravines of jelly, tea, and soda.
It happened several times again, years later,
before they diagnosed the flimsy valve.
She'd wake all sticky, dizzied by a hammering
beneath her breast, as if some desperate thing
were trapped inside of her and wanted out.

I've held a human heart and cut apart
its muscled walls and felt the rubbery strands
that fasten lengthwise to each ventricle.
Its cold potato-heft, wet, veined, and gnarled—
this chunk of love, of passion—seemed petite
and unimpressive, like weird butcher's meat,
or bleak foodstuff for starving pioneers.
I laid it gently back into the hull
of opened ribs, into the gray cadaver
whose face I kept concealed with dampened cloth.

Nowadays, my mother never mentions
her shadow-thoughts—except for once this Christmas:
"Remember how I talked, how sad I was?"
I nodded, glad myself that she no more
sees hints of death graffitied everywhere,
can once more play dismissive symbiote
to that dumb pump, forget how intimate
it sits between us while I lean to hug her
and feel it beating, measuring what's fleeting.

Palinopsia

Disorder of visual perception in which visual
phenomena persist after the actual stimuli are gone

And love brought forth this symptom of disease—
the way her figure burned and wavered there,
still hesitating, combing her wet hair
while he whispered, *Listen, darling! Please!*,
although he knew she'd left and slammed the door.
He took to be the imprint of desire
the way her image clung to him entire
minutes afterwards. This deep rapport
of heart and mind did not suggest a lack
of neural inhibition in the brain
but rather served as visual refrain,
or a love song that his eyes kept playing back,
until the afterimages all blurred
to maddening ghosts that never spoke a word.

Teleopsia/Pelopsia

Disorders of visual perception in which objects
appear much farther away or much closer than
they actually are

It seemed wrong-ended how she looked at things—
the way her fingers' prestidigitation
suggested independent animation,
her fluttering hands the Ms of seagulls' wings,
or how the text all melted on a page,
and then the page seemed wholly out of reach,
as if while she'd been stranded on a beach
the tide had tugged away her means to gauge
the nearest distances, the proximate;
and so his absence now seemed intimate.
The world inverted wrecked her sense of scale;
the emptied moon became a fingernail,
each jagged star a comfort she could seize,
her face warmed to the bone by galaxies.

Prosopagnosia

Inability to recognize faces; face blindness

And what devotion then could recognize
the lover even when his face belies
his very face? Across the wine-dark water,
a man returns from years of distant slaughter,
blistered by salt and wind and wearing rags.
He coughs, he limps, his body's rigging sags,
and when he lands only the dog is there
to nuzzle at his knees and weave the air
with the question mark of his old, grateful tail.
The widow at her loom who might as well
have been unspooling strands of memory
will gaze at him and see, but fail to see,
then come to know the man she felt was dead
as darkness laps against their anchored bed.

AKINETOPSIA

Impairment of visual perception of motion

The world became a broken movie reel
on which a stuttering length of time was wound,
so, like a bat, she learned to move by sound
unless it was a space she knew by feel.
A businessman who whisked by in his suit
seemed frozen as a still-life bowl of fruit;
the swollen river sluicing through its vein
appeared to have been painted for a scene.
And so to ricochet through everything
that rearranged itself in clipped degrees,
the passersby who formed a clever frieze,
she sang to hear the distance echoing,
and found she only suffered for the lack
of silence that did not come bouncing back.

ACHROMATOPSIA
Absence of visual perception of color

The world was Kansas-gray. The tepid sun
had steeped too long within its mug of sky,
and now the lukewarm air was overdone.
The bland horizon line seemed hung awry,
and all the scraps of tree and brush were brown;
so too the house, its shutters falling down,
the grizzled uncle, slurping at his plate,
the girl a pale worm wriggling toward the gate.
It made one welcome how the clouds drew in
and darkened everything, the sirens yelling,
branches swept up in that plume of wind
as if this were the black-and-white foretelling
of Technicolor dreams that would replace
each mushroom with a witch's emerald face.

THE MUNCHKIN CORONER RETURNS TO OZ

Meinhardt Raabe (1915–2010)

At last remains only that old ache—
the longing for an elsewhere out of reach.
Reunion parades with crowds clapping
were no balm. Rustling my blue robes,
I'd feel my breath ratcheting.
After all the world a blur of skirts
at eye level, crotches I spoke to
and made a lowly math of, each
one a face to be recognized, still I was *wee*.
Itty. Give me Culver City. Oz, glittering.
The cameras, Judy Tom-Thumbing me
with weird teenaged mother-love
down to the pith, to my little plum pit
heart, kneeling with a box of chocolates,
cooing *sweets to the sweet*,
pink sleepyheads yawning,
a Munchkin chorus line, the brick road spiraling.
Four lines I learned to sing, hymn-like,
and rewind. But oh, I must aver,
most sincerely, it's the plight
of striped stockinged legs limp
beneath the pitched house, hint
of dead witch that sets me weeping.
Somewhere over there,
give me more heel-clicking.
In The End, I learn to trace
the return-wish backwards:
If I only had. A tornado. A home.
There's no place.

And what if love was better in the days
when making it was fierce as a disease?
Love shuddered nightly in a gauze of sweat,
clenching its waxen water-lily-face
while rain perspired down grimy windowpanes
and blackened walls exhaled their sweet, hot breath.
Pale ladies sat on settees sewing things,
and men in slick galoshes blew white rings,
stuffing their trembly hands into their pockets.
Wheezing, they read lines of poetry,
then knelt by firelight in the drawing rooms
and sputtered wet words straight into the skirts
of their beloveds, whose bright needles dropped.
All was still—a rustle in the quiet
and then each lady sighed and lifted up
her supplicant. She nodded. They both coughed.
There bloomed brilliant carnations in their throats
that petalled their clean pillows red each morning.
They burned alive. They ached but could not eat,
and bore bruised poppies in their hollow cheeks.
Clutching and tumbling, quick and bright and fast
they wrote fresh lines, and kissed and quoted Keats,
dabbing their wrists with phlegm and blots of ink,
then sank together in their present sheets
until the creeping tide of one long sleep
seeped into the sponges of their chests.

Sometimes the gentlest patient
in the Emergency Room
is from the city prison.
This one too—soft-voiced,
lifting his large dark eyes.
He whispers, "Yes, ma'am,"
shy as a deer,
young and brown-skinned
with loosely muscled limbs
gangling off the bed.
His clean, uncoiled anatomy
is almost embarrassing against
pus & pannus, abscess & scarred vein—
everyone bearing his body
like some separate, stricken animal,
its disappointments inevitable.
It seems impolite for us to notice
the fact we are the same age,
his silver handcuffs, track marks,
the inefficiency of my exam,
a rising smell of hot dung
from the old lady in the next bed.
Once, when realms were not distinct—
celestial and earthly—
angels visited, god-wed
women ministered, bathed the feet of sinners,
doe muzzled the saints' hands—
and this would be the moment
of cloud-break revelation.
There are no figs or honey here,
just betadine and isopropyl pads.

DEFECT

Lolling a glossy head that's way too fat,
the infant sags like pudding. His crossed stare
seems alien and flat. The MRI
shows river rock, a polished stone, the smooth,
unspeaking contours of a cool, white egg.
Tracing hieroglyphs, coarse cavern scrawl,

the mute encephalograph purls out its line,
an undulating strand of ink that reads:
lichen, meal worm, toad stool, jade-green moss,
crouched fiddlehead. The baby doesn't blink.
Limp arms, un-kicking feet—he can't translate
to movement. Puddle-black, his eyes are blank.

His wealthy family from the Middle East
glides, dark-eyed, glittering, with scarves and servants.
With translators, a maid, and gilt tea service,
they mutely offer hot cups to the doctors,
tired teams of residents, and medical students.
Veiled, bowing, faceless strangers pass us sweets
of papery phyllo dough, chopped nuts, and honey.
Apologetically we take it, knowing
no one can do anything, there's nothing—
but then the mother speaks. She's lovely, young,
and gestures to her breasts. The lustrous folds
of fabric shift, revealing tears of milk.
A man translates, "She says he understands it
when she feeds him, that he gazes in her face
and sees her." We nod silently, well knowing
the baby's blind. When seizures lightning through
his heavy, milk-fed body, he contorts,
and crying, she beats a fist against her temple.

Our brains, behind their sutured calcium,
are trenched with secrets. Vermiculated whispers
go crackling through those wet, electric forests.
And yet within the gray-white convolutions,
our eloquence of furrow, groove, it's simple—
the answer we articulate is silence.

AFTER A MOLAR PREGNANCY

Little no-child, wicked womb-fruit,
I grew you in your muscle suit,
my hidden chamber. There was blood,
cold jelly, sonograms: I understood
what you were not. Imposter,
snow blur on the screen, yet faster
than a baby fattening, you crept,
a boneless nightmare, while I slept,
and gobbled at the pith of me.
You blew my belly to its tympany;
with tissue fistfuls, clustered grapes,
shaped my silhouette—it apes
a fecund one, a waiting mother.
But you are no one, and no other
life is housed here, doleful mess
of giddy blebs, translucent flesh,
yet still I listen carefully and murmur
nothings to your ghostly human brother.

ASCITES

Abnormal accumulation of serous fluid in the
spaces between tissues and organs in the cavity
of the abdomen

The woman pale in bed
barely lifts her heavy head.
Her belly shines. It's grown
taut and round as a balloon.
Once she's cleaned and draped,
we flex long tubing shaped
like a slender drinking straw,
pierce her side, and slowly draw
clear golden fluid out
into the o-shaped mouth
of a waiting vial.
Like the perennial
lit wick of desire
that furthers its own fire,
once done, the act's reversed,
but it's the opposite of thirst
she suffers from. A font
within her with a want
for liquid springs keeps filling up
her body's fevered cup
with the nectar of the gods—
a fluid still at odds
with mortals, sacred poison
to the merely human.

The Shooter

Emergency Room, East Baltimore

The testicle, unshucked and glistening,
makes us wince, but loses mystery,
a blood-streaked white against the dark skin
of this wild-eyed, weirdly silent kid.
Fifteen. The gentle shoulders, baby face.
His mama holds her head and starts to sway.
The room is full. Urology housestaff
lift that unshelled hard-boiled egg, inspect
its bluish contours in the light like jewelers,
prepare to sew it back into its purse
of scrotal skin. He turns and grimaces
into green waves of rumpled scrubs and faces,
insisting still he must've gotten hit
leaving the store with sodas for his friends.

But one gruff IV tech points out the hole's
through his pocket, mutters, "How about
that for classic. Too ashamed to tell
the truth. He shot himself, dumb boy. The hell
if mine'll run around here playin' thugs."
They frown and help his mother to a seat.
Her shoulders shake, her slippers now are wet
with flecks of blood and squirted saline fluid.

No one standing here has said aloud
how a leg of his hangs limp, immobile,
how this denuded capsule on the thigh,
and the testicle spilled out like oyster meat,
primordial, exposed, and slippery,
unsettle and yet focus us to task.
He turns, big-eyed, to his shivering mom,
"Don't cry. It doesn't hurt yet. I'll be fine."
I wonder why he isn't sobbing, too

as he observes this room, his wound—endures
his nakedness, the pain. The lovely nurse
with a Southern accent and big bosom
takes his soft, child's hand and leans towards him,
then, turning to me, gestures that I take
his other hand. She stands there humming, says,
"You a grown man now—a real, grown man."

IV

A mother knows when daughters are too close.
I felt it from the start, how their new limbs
folded too-tight—wet moth wings or paper fans.
I knew their milky foreheads pressed each other
as they floated there like prayerful fruit,
their seahorse-selves stretching my self to silk.
I heard their private whisperings,
not the normal deep-sea language of twins,
but something tense, high-pitched
like dolphins' cries against tuna nets.
Their fingers curled and uncurled, tiny
sea cabbages, always holding one another,
their salty lips blooming into a kiss,
perpetual, insistent. I felt their half-plum hearts
shushing each other, felt the flex
of their shared shelf of hip, the tide of each flip.
Their very wombsong was plaintive,
the wordless keen of kelp, a whelk's mourning.
I bore them like I bore an underwater urn
planted inside me, raining my own tears
onto the moonscape of my belly
for them to listen. The half-shells
of their lids stayed shut, blind to my plush reds.
And when finally the doctor wrenched
them out, sleek bluish fish, I saw
translucent brows furrow, how they cast
only one misshapen shadow, and I wanted them
unhinged, cast off, thrown back.

Years passed, and they were gone,
but even now I feel their weight
ripping me in two when I dare touch

that empty four-sleeved Sunday dress,
when my heartbeat double-mutters to itself,
or when the gibbous moon turns to watch me
with one of its pale faces.

Springtime. You were gone. I wondered why
your name appeared as birds across the sky,
and every dripping tree that bent to touch
my dripping face touched gently. There was such
a quiet to the dog left on its chain,
a blackness to the asphalt from the rain,
that suddenly I thought the world forgot
and washed you all away—but you had not
dissolved, I saw, reading the thick, knobbed roots
that spelled out words you'd said. The fine green shoots
of grass beneath my fingers felt like hair,
and as I grasped the dirt, I smelled you there.
I saw you in the latticework of stars,
the moon's cheek splotched with all its ancient scars.

ANIMAL AFTERLIVES

They were right, the ancient dreamers,
to tell myths around the hunting fires,
dream on bits of smoked meat their secret names
and animals their ancestors became,
then chalk outlines of elk or eagles in their caverns—
for I've seen it here in modern
podunk western North Carolina.
Take my great-grandmother:
with a trailer full of tufted cockatiels,
she was all birdsquawk, gnarled talons,
and white fluffed hair herself.
Blinking small, dark eyes, she'd cock her near-deaf head,
homing in on twelve-cent figurines,
her world of saltshakers and prayers on china plates.
Plastic friends from the nativity and a few reindeer
waited yardside year-round.
Days spent pecking through coupons and Cheetos,
aviary shit and seed hulls, all revolved
into one seasonless season.
The gold god-voice of the Home Shopping Channel
warbled at a constant pitch above the beaked chatter.
And I declare she was a feathered terror,
wobbling on her skinny, scaly legs,
screeching and ataxic in her nightgown.
Surely she titters somewhere now,
a perfect mimic who never left this world,
flittering near soda cans and shopping center shrubs,
raised into an afterlife of birds.

A giant hand unclenched and scooped the brothers
whirring seedpod-gentle through the sky.
Its calloused mate swept up the tumbling mother
and the father—so they didn't die.
They lifted, circled, grazed a gabled rooftop,
found that they could flap their arms and fly—
in fact, the hand was just a strong air current,
but warm and firm. They liked the world on high,
so chose to stay there, twittering like starlings,
hollow-boned, remote, and passerine.

We're groundlings with binoculars and field guides,
ceramic angels dusty on our shelves.
Outdoors, we search the clouds for missing persons,
although still bound by gravity ourselves.
Necks craning, stiff, we bow our heads. The gloaming
covers dull terrestrial shapes; the trees
are clotted even darker with small mammals
who cluster to sheer silent harmonies.
The nightjar sifting bracken, calling, watches
us walk back to the doorway, listening, stalling.

FOXES

They appear, faces sly as a person's,
perfectly still. To be watched
by a fox is something else,
not supernatural—unless perhaps
these are the other selves
of people lost in woods
returning now to snuff the ground,
black-eyed and red-furred,
quick with an animal-knowledge,
long noses low to forest floor.
Where is the little girl
who wandered off and wasn't found,
or the outdoorsman who clutched his chest
and fell? They are foxes now—
you whisper this, and I'll believe.
I've heard the muffled language in their bark,
felt their old human longings flare
as they've turned to leave.

After smoke and censer, heavy hides pulled back
to reveal our pallets, after the sleeping pill
of ceremony, you've dreamed yourself into a bat,
while I've become an anteater. In the pit
that's slumber, delta waves lap against our totems.
You flap forward, spurt guano, beady-eyed echolocator.
I'm ground-slung, fur-booted, toothless, slow-motile,
snuffing through dust with my eyes lowered. Later,

when we've lost the past, each other, learned our bodies,
we hold little in common: a taste for insects,
temperature. You roost. Your thousand-eyed squad sees
my plumed tail in the cave. I snort hoarse syllables, shake
cataleptic air, think: *coffee cup, toothpick, earring*—objects
to summon you alone, restore our human shape.

TICK

Tiny leaper-off-weeds, quick tooth-seed,
claw-mouth, blood-red beetle-bead
latching to feed near the salt of a vein
until you fatten to coin size. No pain
accompanies you, little bite-fleck, mouth-mote.
You're incidental, even as you sup and bloat,
a misplaced dot smeared into ink blob,
miniscule skin-emperor, vampire-glob.
When you've nestled in an armpit or burrowed in my hair,
I've felt a wrong new button sewn securely there
and nearly screamed—you, the terror of teensy things
with your bleak-black shield and hard lack-of-wings.
You exist, oft-missed punctuation mark
of buggish nightmare sentences, bringer of the dark
caesura, king creeper, lord crawler. I admire at least,
carnivorous incarnadine miniature beast,
your single-minded suckered purpose. Or the fact
that you alert us there are always
happenings we cannot see and days
filled unbeknownst to us with angel-insect-devil
dancing beyond sense's scope, below eye level,
and that's how you,
small sticky-jawed glue,
head of pin, heavy and heme-full,
suggest gods or black magic,
belief's bitty uptick,
awe of invisible.

PERSONALS

I

You, the moon; me, the sun.
You, the steam off jasmine tea;
me, the radio from another room.
Come and listen to me.

II

I won't lie. I'm tired and lonely
and tired of being lonely
and tired of bearing the rough beast
of myself, its dull slump,
through the world with nothing
but bemused, witty ironies.
We can talk over dinner, awkwardly.

III

October on the prep school lawn,
and the girls are playing soccer.
The late light skims their faces;
the ribbons on their ponytails flutter;
they pump their tawny arms
across the green yard.
See the whites of their jerseys,
the long line of their leg muscles.
I am old, too old to join them,
I wasted youth on self-consciousness.
Mature man seeking eighteen-year-old.

IV

I saw you in the grocery store.

We had a conversation—
Remember? The carrots in my hand?
A box of cereal, some fruit, my crooked tooth?
I think you smiled at my poorly told joke,
but I didn't get your name.

V

Divorced mother of two,
kind heart for strays
and brute men who
remind me of my ex-husband.
Rough voices, hard hands,
the lulling presence of their hate.

VI

Picture me at seventeen on a beach with friends.
Late summer: slim, fine tan shoulders.
I ran like the wind and loved books, travelling,
the motown from my brother's stereo,
and flowers dripping in the flower stands.
I swear, I was beautiful then and loved so many things.
Attractive middle-aged woman,
interests wide-ranging.

VII

I could write you many words
but you wouldn't understand.
She died two years ago. That's all.
My friends made me place this ad.

VIII

Ache me like a bad tooth,
or a roaring ear infection,
pain beyond its source,
so that the whole world throbs
with the pulse of ragged nerve
like music, a long cry from the gut,
a love song.
Call me. I want to hear your voice.

IX

Lovely older woman, the metallic prism of your hair, well-cut,
your smooth chin and firm calves, the pressed and tailored suits.
I want to press your soft threads, unloose the bright scarf at
        your throat.
You drink black coffee and read *The Washington Post*.
You wear no ring.
I'll touch your toes beneath the sheets,
and catch the moment when you sing.

X

You, a prayer mumbled one afternoon;
me, candlesticks in paper.
You, the burnt scent of a match;
me, your intercessor.

October Inlet Wedding

Leaf-gilded salt air closed around the porch
where we all sat in rows of folding chairs
waiting for our friend, the sheepish bride,
who hated all things bridal but had said
that this would simplify her health insurance.
Now she stood with flowers in her hair,
an oyster-colored dress her mom had altered,
and tears streaming the gullies of her face.
The skinny, bearded groom rocked on his heels,
aching with a smile, while all the birds
lifted like an afghan off the grass.
They clustered and rewove into the trees,
their feathers charcoal-dark. Their small throats
were resonant, discordant, set to caw
and fluster brush throughout the ceremony.
The rent-a-preacher droned; one sister spoke;
the little, shuffling, half-deaf daddy read
words none of us could hear and yet we clapped,
while late mosquitoes bit our arms and knees,
red chiggers and no-see-ums climbed our legs.
When they forgot and fell into each other
to kiss, the ebb in their self-consciousness
enveloped in the gloaming, bugs, and birds.
Those workaday swamp mutterers; their plainsong.

Navel-Gazing

The baby, bath-time belly glistening, shows
his center mark, that cicatricial gash
the mystics contemplated as a rose,
omphalic core, a mandala. He'll splash
bright soapy rings and circlets in the tub.
His tummy glints round nuclei of light.
Leaning towards her slippery son to scrub,
the mother thinks of buds or seeds, the tight
and knotted body of an unhusked snail
when her hands glaze his perfect belly button.
And then he laughs, his small mouth like a bell.
She feels the resonance, its spreading sudden,
and reaching for the towel, feels the pull
of love like fossil pools—deep, umbilical.

Biographical Note

Joanna Pearson is the winner of the 2012 Donald Justice Poetry Prize and the 2014 Towson Prize for Literature. Her collection of short stories, *Every Human Love*, was published with Acre Books in 2019. She lives in North Carolina with her husband and daughters.